No Contact Rule

How to Get the Guy, Without Giving it Up!

Table of Contents

Introduction

Break ups are hard. That is a universal truth. They become even worse when you believe the person that broke things off with you is the One. When we are in a romantic relationship with someone, our partner often is not just a lover, but our best friend, too. So what do you do when the person that you have spent all your time with for the past year, five years or even a few months suddenly disappears from your life?

You may think that things are over for good, and this may send you into a spiral of despair. Perhaps if you could go back in time, you would do anything to change things so that you and your, now, ex-partner would never have had to part. Time machines have not been invented as yet, but there are other alternatives to get the possible love of your life back into your arms. In this book, we will discuss one of the most tried and true methods to get your ex-lover back to where you think he or she belongs -- with you.

The method that we will focus on is known as the No Contact Rule. The phrase "no contact" paired with the word "rule" may cause a lot of questions to surface in your mind. You may panic at the implication that you will not be able to contact the person that you want to speak to the most right now: your ex. While No Contact can be scary to think of at first, it can make all the difference in how you recover from your break up, how you move forward and whether or not you and your ex will be able to work things out for the better.

In this book, we will explain what exactly the No Contact Rule is, and how you can use it to mend your relationship. We will also talk about how to use the No Contact Rule in situations in which it may seem impossible to keep from coming into contact with your ex. In this book you will also learn why you should stay away from the person you hope to reunite with and how doing so will work to your advantage.

In addition, you will get some ideas as to how to improve your life and occupy your time during the no contact period and how to stay focused on the bigger picture and the overall goal while trying to accomplish the difficult feat that No Contact can be. Finally, you will understand how to tell if your efforts are proving fruitful and in the instance that they do not, what your next steps might be.

So keep reading on to Chapter 1 and let's get started on the next chapter of your life and your relationship. Break ups can be hard, but with the help of this eBook, you'll find a way to make them that much easier.

Chapter 1:

What On Earth Is the No Contact Rule?

You have found yourself on the tail end of a nasty break up which was not your choice. The love of your life just dumped you, and you are left trying to pick up the pieces and figure out where exactly it all went wrong. If you had a time machine, you would go back and change your actions or his or her actions, or do whatever you could so that things just would not end up like this. However, time machines just do not exist yet, and if they do, you don't know about them. What can you do to get the love of your life to change his or her point of view and come back into your open and loving arms? This is where the No Contact Rule comes in.

What is the No Contact Rule?

The No Contact Rule is a simple concept. Basically, it means that you cut off all communication with your ex-partner for a certain amount of time after the break up is final. Using the analogy of a drug, if you have become dependent upon the support of your ex, then the only way to cure this dependency or addiction is to go cold turkey. In many cases, this is the only way to have a clean break.

The next question of course, would be what No Contact entails exactly. Going No Contact means no text messages, no phone calls, no going over to their house, no accidentally bumping into them, no social media connections (including Facebook, Instagram, Snapchat and instant messaging services), no contacting through mutual friends and finally, no subliminal messages or posts "subtly" directed towards your ex on social media sites, such as Facebook.

The No Contact Rule is the same exact concept as quitting something that you are addicted to completely cold turkey. The same way that even a small dose of your drug of choice can get you addicted again, even a small dose of your ex can cause you to become addicted to his or her presence again. One of the great things about the No Contact Rule is that it has been proven to be one of the best ways to get your ex back for the long term.

Why Should You Try No Contact?

There are generally two ways that a relationship can end. It can be a happy break up or a sad break up. There are two situations in which a happy break up might occur. One of those is when both parties agree that there is no longer any real love in the relationship and decide together that they should part ways. The other situation which might lead to a happy break up is if you were the one who decided that the relationship will end, and you are happily single or in another relationship.

On the other hand, there are a couple of situations which may cause a sad break up. The break up will be sad for you if your partner forces you to end the relationship because they are not in love with you anymore, or are dating someone else. If you find that at the end of your relationship, you are sitting at home, lonely, trying to heal your broken heart, stalking your current ex on Facebook, while they are making no secret of having the time of their life, then the No Contact Rule can certainly help you. The fact is that you have to learn to live without your ex, which will be hard to do, especially if your relationship with this person started out as a friendship. This person was probably your best friend.

You might be wondering why you should try to live without your ex if ultimately, your goal is to get back together with this person. The truth is that unless you regain your independence and learn how to live without your ex, you will always come across as desperate and needy to them. Desperation and neediness is synonymous with being unattractive to your ex. They will not want to abandon the freedom of single life in order to return to your dependent ways. In order to get your ex back, you will have to show them that you are independent, happy and confident. The only way to do that is to truly be a happy and confident person, and learning to live with yourself is the beginning.

Another reason why you should give the No Contact Rule a try is that it allows you to be in control of the post break up relationship, which is essential if you are hoping to get back together with your ex. If you have been calling or texting your ex since the breakup, begging with them and pleading with them to take you back, then your ex is currently in control of the post break up relationship. However, if you just stop contacting them, they will have a chance to miss your constant presence in their life and think about you more.

Chapter 2:

3 Exceptional Circumstances That Make No Contact Really Hard (But Not Impossible)

There are certain exceptions in which, no matter how much self-control you might have, and as much as you would like to follow through with sticking to the No Contact Rule, the situation that you and your ex may be in can make it seem impossible to do so. These situations would be ones when it would be impossible to ignore your ex.

You might be wondering if this means that there is ultimately no hope for your ex to be romantically interested in you ever again. However, this is not the case at all. In this chapter, we will discuss some of the situations that can make sticking to No Contact seem impossible, and how you can still make things work in your favor.

Circumstance 1: You Have Children Together

If you and your ex share a child or children, then not contacting them can be very tricky. Of course, you will both want the best interests of your child to come first, even if you have different plans for the ultimate outcome of your romantic relationship.

In this situation, you should strive to be calm, civil and pleasant during any interactions that you must have with your ex. At the same time, try to keep any discussion simple and to the point. If you constantly bring up your feelings every time you come into contact with this person, whether or not it is appropriate for that time, you will completely turn your ex off. In addition, it is very likely that it is not the best time to have a talk about your feelings when dealing with topics or situations related to or in front of your children.

Once you have finished interacting with your ex, and taking care of whatever business needs to be taken care of, you should return to No Contact mode. This means no calling them or texting them unless absolutely necessary, and there is certainly no need to stay in contact with him or her through social media platforms.

Circumstance 2 - You Still Live With the Person

It can be really hard not to be in contact with a person when you have to see them every day, and share a space with them. This situation is probably not the ideal one, but it is not impossible to make No Contact work here. You can still cut off a large amount of your contact with your ex.

In this case, you should aim to be a respectful roommate at all times. Meanwhile, you should keep in mind that you are trying to create a new life for yourself that they are no longer a part of. In this situation as well, you want to keep all conversation short, simple and calm.

Remember, being a respectful roommate means respecting your ex's space and privacy. You are not justified in snooping, looking through their things, or eavesdropping when they have company just because the two of you live together and were previously in a relationship. Should your ex find out that you are violating his or her privacy, you will have an enormously smaller chance of ever appearing attractive to them again.

Circumstance 3 - You Work Together

Another situation in which it may seem impossible to stick to the no contact rule, is if you and your ex also happen to be coworkers. You do not have to quit your job. You come to work to get your work done, so just treat your ex like any other colleague, simple.

Think about the way that you would interact with any other colleague that you might be attracted to. You probably would not have or should not go out of your way to speak to them. Rather, you would go on with your work. Although not everyone will take the same approach, in your case, it is best to consider work as work and use this time to stay focused, bring your "A" game, and shine in your career.

Of course, since you and your ex are coworkers, instances will arise during which you will need to speak to each other. Just be professional, and make sure that the conversation stays related to work matters. This is similar to the example of exes who have children together. Keep all interaction about necessary business, and avoid small talk, emotional discussions and any other contact that is not needed and will undermine your efforts at limited contact.

Other Circumstances to Consider

Perhaps you and your ex used to live together, or spend a lot of time at one another's homes before the break up. This will mean that they will have to make the dreaded visit to reclaim their property from your house, or vice versa. How to approach this in terms of No Contact?

If your ex does call you or come to your home to collect their belongings, you do not have to use the No Contact Rule as an excuse to be a jerk. Rather, you should allow them to get their things, while keeping any conversation short and simple. If they try to bring up the past or the relationship while they are there, do not take the bait. Bring the conversation back to the topic of them getting their things, and keep it moving.

Chapter 3:

The 3 Rules to Live by for the Next 30 Days - Starting Now!

Now that you have a little bit of understanding about what the No Contact Rule is, what it entails, and how you can begin to incorporate it into your life, you may be wondering exactly how long you will need to limit contact with your ex before you start to see results. The answer to that questions is at least thirty days. Of course, if you had an especially bad break up, you can extend this time period to sixty days and even ninety days.

The fact is that both of you will need enough time for the dust to settle around the emotional disaster that you just took part in. Even if your ex initiated the break up, a break up is not pleasant for anyone involved. Time is needed for both parties to redevelop their individuality and reflect on what was good or bad about the relationship. You, as the party who would like the relationship to continue, also need some time to work on yourself and your life, and to reestablish your value. Studies have shown that a thirty day minimum is best for this to fully take place and develop.

So what exactly should you do during these thirty days? In this chapter, we will discuss some of the rules that you can stick to during this time, to make your No Contact mission a success.

Rule #1: No Obsessing Over Your Ex

Of course, if you are definitely still in love with your ex, you will think about them from time to time. That is simply inevitable. However, when you are checking your ex's social media pages first thing in the morning, and every half an hour on the dot throughout the day, then you are not spending your time effectively. Take some time and think about why you are exhibiting this behavior.

The fact is that for many people, the reason behind trying the No Contact Rule is to make their ex miss them and want to be a part of their life again. However, the reality is that even if your ex does miss you and try to contact you, if you have not been doing anything with your time but keeping tabs on him or her, then you have not transformed in any way, and your neediness will come through very clearly. Once they sense this obsession with and dependency on them, they will lose any attraction that was built up during your efforts at no contact.

Remember, the point of the No Contact period is to end your addiction to your ex. You have to go cold turkey in order to do this. If you are checking your ex's Facebook, Twitter, Instagram, etc. every day, then you need to eliminate the source of this little dose of your ex. The best thing you can do is block or delete your ex on social media, or even deactivate your accounts during the no contact period.

Rule #2: Do Not Turn to Alcohol or Drugs

Of course, it is easy to try to use alcohol and drugs to cover the pain that you feel after a break up, in order to try to move forward. Yet, it is important that you realize that this will not heal you in anyway and it certainly will not make you feel better long term. It is like trying to heal a broken bone with a Band-Aid. This does not mean that it is not okay to drink every now and then. In fact, having a couple drinks can be a great social activity that can allow you to spend time with friends, and even get to know new people.

If you are making a habit of drinking, smoking or recreational drug use, however, you are actively decreasing your chances of winning your ex back. Addiction is not a very attractive trait, and in reality, you are just replacing addiction to your ex with another kind of addiction.

Rule #3: Get Out of Your House!

It can be so easy after a break up to succumb to feelings of depression. Television and movies glorify the after break up ritual of laying around in bed all day, never moving to shower or change out of your pajamas, and stuffing yourself with ice cream and other junk foods. It can be rehabilitative to an extent to indulge yourself for a day or two, as you take some time alone to come to terms with your emotions.

However, engaging in this sort of behavior in the long term can be extremely destructive. You will not get better if you spend all of your time isolating yourself from friends and family who offer support, and do not take care of your physical needs. Make it a point to go outside and surround yourself with loved ones. You might be surprised what gems of advice your friends and relatives who have been through the same experience that you are going through have to offer.

Avoid friends who may try to rub your break up in your face due to jealousy or other malicious intentions. Rather, try to make time to spend with those people who will keep you active, engaged and keep your mind off of things that will lead to a repetitive train of thought.

Chapter 4:

Help! What to Do When You Don't Know What to Do

You have fully committed to following the No Contact Rule for a solid thirty days. You have blocked your ex on all social media, deleted their number in your phone and hidden any reminders of the relationship that may be lurking around your home, waiting to send you spiraling. Now what?

It is not uncommon after a break up to feel a gaping hole in one's life where all of the time one used to spend with a significant other was. For instance, if you and your ex had a date night every Saturday, you are used to leaving Saturday nights open, and now you have nothing to do on a Saturday night. Perhaps you two used to spend time together watching the same television shows, and now you cannot watch the show because it is an emotional trigger, but do not know what to do during the time that it airs. We could go on and on looking for places in your life where the absence of your ex seems to be amplified times one thousand, but it is likely that you find instances like these every day.

One of the most important components of the thirty day no contact period is finding oneself, and enjoying one's own company. In this chapter, we will discuss a few things that you can do to replace your partner's presence in your life, as well as when you are feeling the urge to pick up the phone and ruin all of your hard work thus far.

Make Some Changes to Your Outward Behavior and Habits

One thing that you can certainly focus on during the no contact period is making positive physical changes within yourself. There are many things that can cause a break up, but if you cannot help but have a nagging feeling that your ex may have ended things due to becoming less attracted to you over the course of your relationship, now you have plenty of time to work towards changing the image you have of yourself, and in turn the one that they have of you.

Aim to become the sexiest and most attractive version of yourself. You can use this time to get into better physical shape. Exercise releases endorphins which will help to keep your spirits up, and generally feel better about yourself. Try a new sport, start a yoga regimen, join a gym, or pick up a sport that you have always enjoyed again. Do cross-fit training, or even start a jogging routine.

You can also change your image by updating your wardrobe and getting a new haircut. Make sure not to neglect your personal hygiene, and clean up your organs with a better and healthy diet. If you have any bad habits that your significant other had a problem with, for instance, smoking cigarettes, now would be a great time to work on quitting.

Make Intrinsic Changes

Besides changing your outward appearance, it is very important to change the way that you think. Some would argue that becoming stronger mentally is even more important than improving on yourself physically, and it is not hard to see why. One of the most important things that you can accept to change your mindset is that even if you follow the No Contact Rule strictly and perfectly, there is no guarantee that you will be getting your ex back. Accepting this will prevent emotional crashing in the long term if once the thirty days or more have ended, you do not get the results that you were hoping for.

You can also use your time alone to think about why the relationship really ended. Perhaps you will find that you do not really want this relationship back, or that this person was actually not a good fit for you. Many people who have a hard time getting over a break up eventually realize that they are more enchanted with the idea of being in a relationship than the relationship itself. Take some time to reflect on your true intentions.

Cultivate Your Social Life

As mentioned before, it is important to have a good support system in order to build yourself up after a break up. This process cannot be carried out easily alone. Keep your friends close to you during this time, and confide in those that you trust. Let them listen to your concerns, you thoughts and even your worries. When they invite you to get out of the house and spend some time with them, say yes! Force yourself to go out and have a good time, no matter how much you want to stay home and think about the past.

Spending time with your friends will make you realize that you are still loved and still appreciated. It will solidify the idea that your ex is not the only individual in the world that you can look to as a source of approval. This is important, because after being wrapped up in a relationship, and likely only caring if the person you are in love with cared for you, you can easily succumb to feelings of worthlessness after the break up. No matter what happens to you in life, you will always have your friends and that is something that you should be thankful for.

You should also not be afraid to go on a date during the no contact period. Yes, the whole reason that you are not speaking to or contacting your ex in anyway is so that you can get them back, or so it may seem. The fact is that there is so much more to the no contact rule than just getting back your old relationship. Get back out there when you are ready, keeping in mind that going on a date does not mean that you will jump into a new relationship immediately. Rather, going on a few dates will give you an ego boost, and make you feel better about yourself in the long run.

Take Some Time to Relax

So far in this chapter, we have discussed a lot of the things that you should be doing in order to take control of your life, and be more active. This does not mean that you should not take some time to relax and unwind. Breaking up with a significant other is a very hard thing to go through, and you are doing your absolute best to cope with it. Now, more than ever, it is important for you to reward yourself with some rest and relaxation.

Some of the things you should consider doing to relax include a spa day, meditation or even yoga. Splurge and treat yourself to a professional massage or a relaxing bubble bath. Cook yourself your favorite foods, or order your favorite takeout. Give yourself the treatment that you deserve, for surviving one of the hardest things that can happen in life, which is heartbreak.

Chapter 5:

Is It Too Late? Reasons You Should Keep Going

(Or Start Again)

You started off the no contact period on the right track, but temptation called and on a particularly trying night, you sent a text to your ex. What do you do now? The fact is that you have broken the number one rule of the no contact period, and contacted your ex. Is all hope lost? Should you keep trying? In this chapter, we will look at some of the reasons why you should stick to the No Contact Rule and what to do if you slip up.

Why Should You Stick with the No Contact Rule?

It is not uncommon that after a week or so of not contacting your ex, one of two things may happen. You may think that you have spent enough time getting over the break up, and the two of you can talk as just friends again. *Thirty days may be too much*, you say to yourself. *Our relationship is different.* Perhaps you convince yourself that this approach is a waste of time, and the only way to get your ex back is to constantly be in his or her life.

First and foremost, you should understand that both of these lines of reasoning are flawed. It is more likely than not that the rush of speaking with your ex again will open the emotional floodgates, leading to more hurt feelings, broken expectations and disappointment than you may have felt before. There are a few simple reasons why the No Contact Rule works, and why you need to stick it out.

After you have just gone through a break up, you are the most vulnerable version of yourself. You need some time to calm down, sort through your emotions, ease your mind and begin to think with reason and logic. You will not get anywhere if you and your ex continue to talk immediately after the break up, as there will likely be a lot of hostility between the two of you, and this will lead to constant arguments.

You may think that if you disappear from your ex's life, you will disappear from his or her mind completely and open the door for someone to take your place. The fact is that even while you are constantly nagging and begging your ex to come back to your arms, they are looking for other options, and may have already found some as your continue pushing them away with your needy behavior. If you give your ex some room, they will eventually begin to wonder why you are no longer pleading with them, and perhaps they will begin to think of you fondly with feelings of nostalgia for the relationship. In essence, you cutting the cord will give you control over the situation.

Even more so than giving you control over the relationship between yourself and your ex, the No Contact Rule allows you to focus on healing yourself. It is important for you to heal emotionally. Break ups are hard, and if you do not take the time to go through the healing process completely, you will find that you are stunted in your growth and stuck in the same position, rather than blooming and becoming a better version of yourself to make the most out of future relationships.

The No Contact period can also give you time to rebuild a strong foundation for your relationship with your ex, if it is meant to be. Staying in contact with an ex can often lead to the unhealthy loop of the on again off again relationship. We all know that couple that stays together while breaking up every few months and getting back together again after a few weeks. A healthy relationship starts with a strong foundation, not a shaky one, and if you ever wish to recover your relationship with your ex, the no contact period will allow you enough time to start from scratch and build up a strong foundation again.

What to Do if You Break the No Contact Rule

If there is any concept that has been made clear in this book so far, it is that in order to carry out the No Contact Rule correctly, you must cut your ex out of your life completely for no less than thirty days. This is no easy feat, but takes a lot of self-control and discipline. A lot of people who attempt this method do not even last through the first day.

Of course, your mind will be telling you to stay away from any forms of communication with your ex, while your heart begs you to just open your text messaging app and type "Hey". When you break No Contact, no matter if it is by doing something as simple as sending a text message, you relinquish your control and power over the situation, which is the worst thing you can possibly do at this stage.

Breaking the No Contact Rule in any way, shape or form means that you have to start again from day one. Even if you have made it fifteen days without contacting your ex, and on the sixteenth day you give in and send them a Facebook message, you have to go back to the beginning. The fact is, that in order for this process to have the desired effect, you have to prove to yourself that you can go for thirty full days, at least, without relying on your ex for anything.

Chapter 6:
Exceptions –
When, and Only When

Of course, there are exceptions to every rule, and the No Contact Rule is not an exception to that one. There are certain instances in which you are allowed to go outside of the strict guidelines of the No Contact Rule and in this chapter, we will discuss exactly what those exceptions might be.

You Have Been Broken Up for a While

One instance in which the No Contact Rule may not be as effective is if it has been months since your break up. If you and your ex have been in contact during this time the No Contact can still be an effective way of reigniting the relationship. The time away will give both of you enough space to think about what you really want from each other. It will also have the same effect of helping you to develop as an individual without being dependent on conversation from your ex for your emotional and mental wellbeing.

At the same time, if you and your ex broke up some time ago and have not really spoken much since that time, No Contact may not have the desired effect. Simply put, if you have not been contacting each other, your ex will not feel or notice a difference if you decide to extend your silence to a month or two. They may just figure that you have moved on. This is why in this situation, No Contact may be trick, and possibly not the best solution.

You Have to Have Some Form of Contact with Your Ex Due to the Nature of Your Relationship

As discussed in chapter two, when you and your ex live together, it can be hard to follow no contact completely. Remember, limit unnecessary contact, without making it obvious that you are trying to avoid them. When you do address your ex, do not act sad, angry or emotional. Be friendly and polite, and cut the conversations short as soon as possible. Say something like you have made plans with some friends and you do not have time talk right now. You should seem to be embracing the freedom of being single. Again, having to see your ex at work or school regularly can complicate things as well. Having children together will also make it impossible to avoid contact all together. Limit conversation to topics related to the children. Do so with a positive attitude and do the best you can to keep the conversation away from emotionally intense topics, or issues related to your relationship.

You Are Going Through a Divorce

If you and your ex are going through a divorce, it may be impossible to retrieve your relationship with your ex. The process of filing for, going through and finalizing a divorce is much more complex and concrete than simply calling things off as boyfriend and girlfriend. If your ex has already spent money on a lawyer and taken the legal steps necessary to end your marriage, it can take a lot more than just the No Contact Rule to get them to reconsider their actions.

Your Ex Contacts You

When your ex is constantly contacting you, it can be hard to maintain no contact. Make sure that they understand that they have to choose between being in a relationship with you or not having you in their life at all. This may seem harsh, but when someone that you have spent so much time with is suddenly gone from your life, it can be overwhelmingly painful.

If your ex is sending you a message just to chat, you do not have to respond. You can tell them that you are busy. However, if the message is about something important, you can respond in a few hours, with an upbeat and friendly manner and as briefly as possible. Maybe your ex is telling you that they miss you and are sad when you are not around. If you are getting mixed messages, the thirty days of no contact can help you to decode what exactly your ex's goals are in terms of your relationship.

Chapter 7:

Is It Working? Tips and Tricks for Staying on Track

You are halfway through the no contact period, and you may be wondering whether all of your efforts are going to waste. How do you tell whether or not the No Contact Rule is working for you if you cannot speak to your ex to figure out where his or her mind is in terms of you and your relationship together? In this chapter, we will look at a few ways to figure out whether or not it is working so far, and to keep you focused on your goal so that you do not feel compelled to lose your self-control in the final stretch.

Looking for Signs That No Contact Is Working

Many people will try to look to their ex for signs that the No Contact Rule it working. For instance, one may ask questions like "Is my ex reaching out to me?" "Why hasn't he or she contacted me yet?" "Does he or she miss me?" However, the fact is that the No Contact Rule is something that you do for yourself, and so the answer to the question of whether it is working or not is something that you will have to search for within.

One sign that it is working is that you are feeling much better emotionally, no longer driven by negative emotions such as range, anger, depression, desperation of neediness. You have exited the era of crisis that takes place inevitably after a break up period, and are ready to take on life as a whole and self-sufficient individual, and do things with your life moving forward.

Another sign that the No Contact Rule is working for you is that you actually love yourself and your life. Sometimes you are moving forward and doing things that you may not want to do just for the sake of eventually getting back together with your ex. Instead, you are spending more time focusing on yourself, not centering your life on your ex. You are no longer waiting by the phone hoping that your ex is going to call, afraid to go out and live life because you might miss out on the chance to speak to that person.

You can also tell if the No Contact Rule is working if you are taking care of yourself, feeding yourself nutritious food and exercising to keep your body and mind in good shape and you have confidence in yourself. You are no longer living in that purgatory in which anything that your ex says will dictate your responses or actions in life. You are not waiting for compliments from this person so that you can feel good about yourself, and if he or she says something negative about you, you do not feel worthless, as you now understand your own worth.

The fact is that becoming this person as a result of the No Contact Rule, when you and your ex are considering getting back together you will be the best possible version of yourself, and even more attractive. Even if your ex does not regain romantic feelings for you, you will be in the best shape to move forward and find someone who can appreciate you for the treasure that you are, have been and have become.

Tips for Staying Focused

One thing that will help you to stay on track when employing the No Contact Rule is your mentality about the purpose of this exercise. For many, the goal of using the No Contact Rule is to get your ex to miss you and want to be with you again. While this is one of the primary goals, and why many people turn to the No Contact Rule, it is important to realize that all of the time spent cutting yourself off from this person is an opportunity to improve yourself.

The fact is that at the end of the thirty day, sixty day or even ninety day period, you and your ex may not be able to reconcile. You may be surprise to find that the new you has realized that this is no longer something that you are interested in! So, you did not talk to your ex for months and you may wonder "What do I have to show for this?" Well, if you follow the advice given in this book, you should have a better mind, body and social life to show for it.

You will have taken time to sort through your emotions and thoughts and heal and contacting your ex before you have had enough time to give yourself the emotional and physical care that you need could derail this entire process and leave you in a rut that will be hard to climb out of as long as you continue to depend on your ex and their love to make you the person that you want to be. If you stay focused on the fact that the No Contact Rule can bring you to the realization of more than one goal, you will not lose your determination to stick to it.

Chapter 8:

Scenarios - Preparation is Your Friend

One of the most important things to do when using the No Contact Rule is to manage your expectations. Many will read this information and close this book with the belief that No Contact is a guarantee that by the end of the no contact period, your ex will be calling you nonstop, you will have so much control of the situation that he or she will come crawling back to you and be eating out of the palm of your hand, or that it will be easy to reestablish a relationship with your ex. The truth is that while it is very possible that these things might happen, it is also possible that things will not go this way at all.

If you go into this exercise believing that these things will happen and that there will be no other outcomes, then you will be depressed and disappointed if this does not happen at all. In fact, many people who do the No Contact Rule get depressed if they do not hear from their ex at all during the no contact period. If you do not prepare yourself for all of the possible scenarios that could take place as a result of you doing the No Contact Rule, this could be you.

Preparing for Your Ex's Reaction to the No Contact Period

It could be possible that the No Contact Rule is actually working on your ex, but he or she is really good at hiding the emotions that they might be feeling. Perhaps they are embarrassed about making the wrong choice and ending their relationship with you. Whatever the case might be, not contacting your ex is just the beginning of the process, and there is no point in getting depressed about something that has not had time to fully develop.

Instead, go into the No Contact Period with the mindset that if your ex contacts you that would be great, but if they do not then it is their loss. If you have this mentality then you will do well when it comes to the bigger picture of the no contact rule. If you have a mentality of being depressed and waiting for a phone call, you will not progress, as your life will still revolve around this person, and eventually, even if your ex does contact you, you will fail on a bigger level.

What Could It Mean if Your Ex Has Not Contacted You?

There are many reasons why an ex may not contact you during this period. Some people are very stubborn and their pride will not allow them to be the one to reach out first. For some, getting compliments from a significant other is what they thrive on. They prefer to have their egos stroked, and once they realize that you might be ignoring them, they will see the no contact period as a game. In this game, whoever reaches out first will lose. This means that while a person might be thinking about you constantly, you will have to make the first step and reach out, and once you do this after you have had time to build yourself and grow during the No Contact Period, you may find that you get a favorable response.

Another scenario in which it may seem like the No Contact Rule is working is if your ex is trying to get back at you somehow. When a relationship ends, both parties often become so wrapped up in their emotional reactions that they overlook that the break up could have been just as hard on the other individual. Some people do not like to appear vulnerable by sharing their feelings, so while it is possible that they are hurting from the end of the relationship just as much as you are, it could appear that they are totally and completely unaffected by it.

When people keep negative feelings inside, these feelings can easily develop into resentment and anger, and this could lead to your ex trying to lash out at you to compensate for these negative feelings by not talking to you. You might wonder why your ex would be angry at you if they were the one who ended things. However, some people feel that they are the victim no matter what the case, and even if at the time your ex thought breaking up was best, if they begin to realize that they have made a mistake and along with this that you are not begging for them to come back, they may start to feel as though the tables have turned and they are the ones losing out.

Now the two of you are at a crossroads, because while you are taking time to heal and make yourself better for the possible reconciliation of your relationship, he or she may perceive you as having some kind of antagonistic feelings towards him or her. This will lead to your ex trying to take revenge on you with silence as well, knowing or hoping that their silence will hurt you.

By keeping your eyes on the prize and preparing yourself for any scenario when it comes to the no contact rule, you will be ready for the moment when your ex finally does contact you. Even in the situations described above, it is possible for your ex to break down and contact you even on the last day of the no contact period. Just stay focused and do not think that things are not going to work out when enough time has not yet passed for the dust to settle in your situation. Remember, preparing yourself is the best way to gain a victory.

Chapter 9:

How to Tell When You've Succeeded

(Or Not)

When you have successfully made it through the majority of the No Contact period, you will probably be on the lookout for signs that your ex wants you back, which would mean that on some level you succeeded. As discussed in the previous few chapters, there is more than one signifier of success when it comes to the No Contact Rule. You might also wonder how to tell if the No Contact Rule was not a success for you. In this chapter, we will discuss some signs that your ex is interested in pursuing a relationship with you again. We will also talk about some ways to tell whether in the grand scheme of things the No Contact Rule was a success of failure for you as an individual.

Signs Your Ex Wants to Get Back Together With You

1. They Contact You

This means that you have been on your ex's mind. They still care about you and have been thinking about you if they decide to reach out to your through a phone call, text message or even on social media.

2. They Are Looking For Your Approval

Perhaps they want to share their accomplishments with you. If your ex contacts you to let you know about a promotion that they scored at work, or a good grade that they achieved in a hard course or on an exam, they want you to be a part of their success and care about what you think of them. You should also be on the lookout for what seems like competition on your ex's part. If they share their success in a way that makes you feel that they are making progress a competition between the two of you, while it may seem negative, they still care about how successful they appear to you.

3. Personal Questions

When your ex starts asking personal questions about you and your life, and how you are doing, then they definitely still care for you. They may ask you about a family member that they remember was going through a hard time, or how you are dealing with a situation that they may be aware of. All of these inquiries lead to the fact that they are thinking of you, and want the best for you on some level.

4. They Act Emotional

You may find that your ex is sending you mixed signals and giving off hot and cold emotional messages. This means that they are torn about their feelings for you and that those feelings may be strong. It is important that if this is the case you should try to direct those strong feelings toward a positive direction by exhibiting positive feelings yourself. Eventually, they will make up their mind, and it is very likely that their heart will lead them right back to you.

5. They Physically Touch You

If you and your ex meet up after the no contact period and they reach out to touch you physically, this is a sign that they definitely may still like you. Holding hands, caressing and even playful nudging are all indicators of a need for physical contact, which shows a level of care coming from your ex.

How to Tell if the No Contact Rule Worked for You

If you used the No Contact period to grow into the best version of yourself, whether or not you end this exercise with your ex back in your life for good, the No Contact Rule was a success for you. Remember, No Contact is about so much more than getting your lost lover back. It is about finding the part of yourself that you lost while in a relationship and filling the void that your ex has left with positivity so that you can become a whole and complete person.

At the end of the thirty day period, if you feel happier and complete, and have a clearer mind and emotional state, the No Contact was a success. You may even find that you can be happy by yourself, even with the knowledge that you would love to try again with your ex. Even if you do not get the outcome you had hoped for, you are not depressed or desperate. Rather, you can see that your ex is the one missing out, and cast your line to see who is out there that will be able to see the real you and love everything that you have to offer.

How to Tell if the No Contact Rule Did Not Work For You

One major sign that the No Contact Rule was not a success for you is the absence of genuine happiness. One can attain the goal of getting their ex back using the no contact rule and still find that they are unhappy, eventually leading the relationship to end once again. If you used the time during the no contact period to obsess over your ex, wait for them to call and did not break your dependency upon him or her, your ex may soon realize that you are no different from the way you were before the break up and choose to leave for good this time. Also, if you did not take time to think about what may have been the real cause for the break up so that it could be discussed before embarking on a new relationship with your ex, the same problem or problems will repeat themselves leading to unhappiness and eventually another break up.

If you do not get your ex back with the No Contact Rule, as it has been stressed, you do not necessarily have to be unhappy. However, if you are, then the no contact rule did not work. Whatever the reason may be that your ex has chosen not to try to rekindle a relationship with you, if this outcome causes depression and hopelessness, then it is likely that you did not use the time during the no contact period wisely. Remember, you should have been using this time to grow as a person, and become complete in your individuality. Waiting for your ex to return so that you can feel complete again is the number one way to lead to failure, worsen heartbreak and stunt personal and emotional growth at the end of the no contact period.

Chapter 10:

Now What? How to Move on to a Better Situation (With or Without Him)

We have finally reached the end of our journey through the Dos and Don'ts of No Contact, and you are probably wondering what to do once you have successfully gone through the no contact period and have lived to see the other end. How to approach your ex and discuss perhaps giving things another try? What if he or she does not want to try again? In this chapter, we will discuss some general guidelines for what to do once you have finished the no contact period, and how to move forward with or without your ex.

Before You Make First Contact

Before you contact your ex after taking the time to remove them out of your life, you need to do some reflection to decide what you would like to do moving forward. The fact is that the relationship ended for a reason. If you do not think carefully about what that reason might have been and try to find a solution to the problem, you are setting your relationship up to fail a second time. Can you imagine going through all of this twice? No one wants to imagine that.

In order to prevent that outcome, spend some time trying to figure out why you and your ex broke up in the first place. Once you have discovered the problem, you should be honest with yourself in deciding whether you can resolve the issue and whether you are prepared to do so. Sometimes, it is not possible to fix whatever the problem was. In this case, you and your ex may have to compromise, or accept whatever the issue is and move on. This is not an easy path to take, and it requires commitment and effort from both parties.

Even if you can solve the problem, it does not mean that you are willing to do so. This is where honesty with yourself is important. If it is a simple problem, such as cutting out a bad habit or developing a new habit, then decide whether you are up for the challenge. However, if you see the problem and the solution in its entirety and do not think that you, your ex, or even the both of you have what it takes to come to an amicable solution, then it might be better to try to move on to someone new. Giving yourself time away from the situation with the no contact rule is a great way to reflect with a clear head, free of emotions which can cloud your judgement and lead you into a vicious cycle.

How to Establish Communication After No Contact

After not speaking with your ex for thirty or sixty days, you may be wondering how to get back into the swing of things. You have many options for contact. You can give your ex a call on the phone, to reach out and see how he or she has been. You can also write an email, or just a simple text message to them.

Some guidelines to follow are to keep your message open ended so that your ex will feel comfortable replying. You do not want to start off the conversation by saying something like "Hi, I want us to get back together." This may make your ex feel pressured to give an answer immediately, and even push him or her away. Try just asking how they have been and what new developments have taken place in their lives since the last time that you spoke.

You should also try to do whatever in your power that you can to make it clear to your ex that you do not hate them. Remember, they have not heard from you in a month or more, and the last time the two of you spoke, the circumstances were very emotionally charged. They have no idea of your feelings towards them, so make it easy for them to see that whatever your feelings may be they are not negative.

As time passes, you and your ex will continue to speak more. As your communication grows, you may arrange a time to meet up and talk in person, if they do not suggest it first. Remember, you are starting a clean slate and hoping to rebuild an even better relationship on a new and stronger foundation. Do not rush anything. Just take your time, and if things are meant to work out the way that you want them to, they will.

It is possible that your ex may try to manipulate your emotions in negative ways out of resentment and anger. If this is the case, recognize it immediately and do not stoop to his or her level. The fact is that if they actually did not care about you, they would not have strong feelings towards you, whether negative or positive. As mentioned in the previous chapter, it is important to get those feelings on a positive track, and you encourage this by exuding positive energy yourself.

What If Things Do Not Work Out Between You and Your Ex

If things do not go the way that you had hoped between you and your ex, in terms of he or she choosing not to reconcile with you, do not worry. You are better off for having employed the no contact rule, even with these results. You gave yourself time to properly heal from the sting of a bad break up. You rebuilt your connections with your friends and family, and maybe you even went on a few dates to boost your confidence in yourself. Most importantly, you've learned to love yourself completely, and to live as an individual, without depending on someone else (who might not even appreciate you fully) for compliments and self-esteem.

At the end of the day, No Contact is about you, and if you used this period to become the best possible version of yourself, then No Contact was a success!

Conclusion

Congratulations for making it to the end!

Hopefully you were able to apply the tips in this book to your situation and use the No Contact Rule to repair your relationship with your (soon to be no longer) ex.

Remember that you should exercise the No Contact Rule for a period of at least thirty days in order for it to be effective and bring changes in your mentality and that of your ex. Do not forget that one of the most important things to do during the No Contact period is to work on your physical and mental health, and not to shy away from social development. Rely on friends and family to get through this time, and use the opportunity to grow yourself as a person without them.

Finally, and perhaps most importantly, if you do successfully complete No Contact and your ex does NOT have a change of heart, **it is not the end of the world**. Your time and effort was not wasted as you have rehabilitated and become a better you. Get back out there! You never know where you might find true love!

I hope that you have got as much out of this book as I did sharing it with you and the thousands of other women taking back the power in their relationships. If you enjoyed this book, I would be very appreciative if you could leave me a review on Amazon – so that someone else can benefit from it as much as you hopefully have.

Thank you, and good luck!

Printed in Great Britain
by Amazon